The Real Saint Patrick

The Real Saint Patrick

'. . . He still speaks even though he is dead.'

(Book of Hebrews)

J. M. HOLMES

IRISH HILL
PUBLICATIONS

The Real St. Patrick
Copyright © 2002 J. M. Holmes

ISBN 0-9541807-0-4

IRISH HILL PUBLICATIONS
20 Logwood Road,
Ballyclare,
Co. Antrim,
BT39 9LR,
Northern Ireland.

Printed by Antrim Printers,
Steeple Industrial Estate, Antrim, BT41 1AB.
Tel: 028 9442 8053

~ Dedication ~

To my dear wife, Ella

Acknowledgements

Quotations from Patrick's works are taken, by permission, from R.P.C. Hanson's English translation contained in his excellent book, 'The Life and Writings of the Historical St. Patrick' - New York 1983.

The author is deeply grateful for encouragement and advice given to him by Mrs. Mary Hanson, Mrs. Christine Fleming, Rev. Norman Reid, Mr. George Beale of Stranmillis College, Mr. Stuart O'Seanóir of Trinity College Dublin and Dr. Marie T. Flanagan of The Queen's University of Belfast.

My heartfelt thanks to Mrs. Michelle McCabe of Antrim Printers who worked tirelessly for many hours on the technical details of this book and whose enthusiasm and encouragement were a constant inspiration to me.

A translation of the full text of Patrick's two writings, the 'Confession' (or Declaration) and 'Letter' are included in this book by kind permission of Mrs. Eva Bieler.

Thanks to my son Paul and daughters Deborah, Grace, Esther and Sarah for all their help.

Thanks also to Alannah Hopkin for the wealth of information contained in her book 'The Living Legend of St. Patrick' and for her permission to quote from that book (see page 55).

Irish scenes appearing in this book are from original photographs and sketches by Paul Holmes.

• • •

From the volumes of history John Holmes has brought Patrick to life in a pleasant easy-to-read book which captures Patrick's heartbeat and shows us the man who braved numerous dangers to bring the gospel to pagan Ireland. Here too, we have Patrick's own writings, including his 'Confession'. It deserves wide circulation.
- Rev. Colin N. Peckham,
Principal of Faith Mission Bible College, Edinburgh.

'. . . . it is very welcome to have a book which concentrates on Patrick's own writings and is so free from all the non-historical lore that has become attached to his career.'
- Dr. Marie T. Flanagan,
The Queen's University of Belfast.

Contents

Photographs

Comments on this book
or requests for further information
about St. Patrick are welcome -
the author can be contacted by writing to:

110 Middle Abbey Street,
Dublin 1,
Republic of Ireland

or

20 Logwood Road,
Ballyclare,
Co. Antrim,
BT39 9LR,
Northern Ireland.

Preface

t. Patrick is among the most famous figures in history. He is forever linked, and rightly so, with Ireland and the Irish people. Over many centuries of Irish history no other person has commanded such lasting interest or appealed more to the imagination of the people.

Patrick is the world's best-known patron saint. On the 17th of March each year he is celebrated in a multitude of places around the globe; in New York for example a parade in his honour takes several hours to pass along Fifth Avenue and is watched by millions. Innumerable places, streets, cathedrals, colleges, and institutions carry his name and yet surprisingly few individuals have anything more than a very vague knowledge or understanding of the man himself. You would be hard pressed, it would seem, to find anyone, even in our halls of learning, who could quote something that Patrick has said.

In recent years there has been, among some scholars, a revival of interest in the life of St. Patrick and a number of well researched books have appeared; for a variety of reasons, however, these publications do not appear to have attracted either the interest or the wide range of readers which they deserve.

Visible evidence of Ireland's early Christian community still exists. The sites of former Monastic settlements can be identified, and the impressive ruins of ancient churches, many of them very large, take us back to the 9th or possibly the 8th century. The oldest of the surviving High Crosses may well have been reverently carved from stone in the 7th century. But the Gospel of Christ first came to this land a few hundred years earlier - exactly how and when has been the subject of much speculation and we will never know all the details.

One thing we do know for certain is that the missionary work of the man we call St. Patrick belongs to the 5th century; to times and conditions far distant from ours, yet with strange similarities. Our knowledge of society in Ireland in those days is very limited, for virtually nothing remains of the materials needed to construct some kind of detailed history. By nature of the case it must also be admitted that there is a multitude of questions about Patrick which cannot be answered with complete confidence. Indeed, there is a multitude of questions about him *which can never be answered* -- at least not in this life.

We can however be reasonably certain about many things and there are areas where the scholars are in general agreement: The historical basis of this little book rests on such material.

There is an abundance of literature containing colourful stories about Patrick's exploits -- stories which in actual fact do him an injustice. Hopefully this publication, by concentrating on a simple and factual look at his life, will help to rescue him from much unnecessary glory! Don't let that be a disappointment; the real St. Patrick is more worthy of our attention, more exciting, than any of the fables that have grown around his name.

chapter one

Ðiscovery

orn and reared in Ireland myself, I always had a vague interest in St. Patrick and often when driving through the quiet Antrim countryside the impressive sight of Slemish Mountain would cause my thoughts to turn to this man. Patrick, though, as a person, was to me just a shadowy figure belonging to ancient times and having no real relevance to life today.

There came a time however when I began to ask, 'Who really was St. Patrick? Did he actually exist? What kind of mission did he have in Ireland?' My first step in finding answers was to seek help from the History Department at the Queen's University of Belfast. I was given very useful information and directed to the best literature on the subject. Soon I found myself on a fascinating journey of discovery, one which was to capture my mind, touch my heart, and at times bring me close to tears; a journey which, in a sense, has not yet ended.

It has been said that Patrick received much of his education and religious training on mainland Europe, was sent to Ireland by the Bishop of Rome, landed initially at Wicklow, established a centre of Christian witness, illustrated the doctrine of the Trinity by using a shamrock, was enormously successful, performed a great number of miracles, overcame the opposition of the High King at Tara, climbed to the top of Croagh Patrick to commune with God, died on the 17th of March and was buried at Downpatrick in Co. Down.

While certain parts of this information may be more acceptable than others, the truth has to be faced that none of these 'facts' has any real *historical* credibility. Evidence of a kind does indeed exist for some of the details given but little importance can be given to it if we are on a search for the real person. Patrick died somewhere in Ireland about the year 460 AD but we have no knowledge of the place or the circumstances of his death. Some 200 years or more later a man called Muirchú and a cleric named Tírechán both produced writings proposing to give details of the life and travels of St. Patrick. Like other so called 'Lives' that followed, these books are dominated by tedious accounts of most unconvincing miracles and it is possible to detect in them that Patrick's name has been used to obtain advantage in the politics of religion. While they do contain some elements of truth they are no longer taken seriously and if they contained all the information available we could be pardoned for wondering if Patrick ever existed! Perhaps the main value of these books may be in the way they confirm, *by contrast*, the truth of the sober words and modest claims of two other, more ancient, documents.

During those dark years after his decease, in the providence of God, somehow, somewhere in Ireland, two works of Patrick himself were reverently preserved and copied. These two writings, 'The Letter to Coroticus' and the 'Confession' are judged to be absolutely authentic -- *they are historical documents of incredible value.* Patrician studies in recent years have seen the gradual but positive rejection of all legendary material and among scholars these two works, while always accepted as genuine, are now acknowledged to be the only substantial source of information on the life and character of St. Patrick. *They are, by far, Ireland's oldest literature* and are about the only known Latin writings of that age to have come out of a country of the Barbarians, that is, outside the boundaries of the Roman Empire.

In addition to these there exist some other writings which are credited to St. Patrick but for the most part it can easily be shown that they belong to a much later period in history. Included among these is a famous poem known as 'The Breastplate of St. Patrick.' Originally written in Irish it is associated with the early Celtic church and is a very beautiful work but was almost certainly not composed by Patrick.

A later chapter will examine in more detail the 'letter' and the 'confession' but again we emphasise that almost all that can reliably be said about Patrick is based on painstaking research into conditions pertaining in the fourth and fifth centuries and, *more especially,* on what he himself has said. So who was St. Patrick?

chapter two

Early Days

atrick was a Briton. He was brought up in the latter days of the Roman occupation: few appreciate the fact that *he is the only native Briton of that era that we really know anything about.* To give a date for his birth is impossible but it was probably near the end of the fourth century -- 390 AD has been suggested. Records of those days are scant but there is reason to believe that the Christian faith had spread widely in Britain and Patrick certainly came under its influence. He was of an aristocratic, prosperous, and religious family. His father Calpornius, in addition to being a 'deacon' in the church, held an official position associated with the Roman administration and owned a villa and estate near to a village called Bannavem Taberniae (there is some doubt about the exact name). The location of that village has never been established but almost certainly it lay near the West coast of Britain. Patrick's native tongue was an old Celtic language of which the present day Welsh is a modified form.

Being among the privileged classes, he would also have been familiar with Latin.

He has given us few details of his childhood and early teens but does suggest that with regard to Christian influences he was rebellious and had turned his back on God.

One fateful day a party of fierce Irish raiders descended on the estate; some of the servants were murdered and sixteen year old Patrick, along with many others, was overpowered, dragged to the boats, and shipped across the sea to a life of slavery in Ireland. It was a frightening, traumatic experience, the memory of which remained with him for the rest of his life.

As they headed home the pagan raiders were not to know, as we know, that their brutal activities that day would change the history of their island nor that, sixteen centuries later, the name of one of the captives huddled in the bottom of the vessel would be a household word, better known than that of Saint Augustine or any of the Emperors of Rome.

Hillside in the West of Ireland

Towards Rathlin

*'The Lord opened the understanding of
my unbelieving heart that I might
recall my sins and turn with all my
heart to the Lord my God.'*

chapter three

Conversion

he treatment of those captured for the slave market would have been anything but humane: Patrick recalls that he experienced 'hunger,' 'nakedness,' and 'being near to the point of collapse.' He was sold and eventually found himself working for a sheep farmer where conditions, initially at least, may not have been much better. Whatever religion he had was of the nominal sort, but now his hopeless and desperate plight moved him to earnestly seek for God.

His search was not in vain - for him, as with many others before and since, the darkest hour was just before the dawn. Alone in Ireland, with no help but the Holy Spirit and his memory of the gospel, he was enduringly converted. To describe such a very personal experience we will be content with gathering together some of his own words on the subject. Up to that time he confessed '... I did not know the true God...' but '...lay in death and unbelief,'

and '...took no thought for my salvation...' Then he said 'The Lord opened the *understanding of my unbelieving heart that I might recall my sins and turn with all my heart to the Lord my God.'*

The reality of that experience was woven into the remainder of his life. Near the end of his career, casting an eye back, he could say that from that time on '...the love of God and the fear of Him have grown in me and up to this day by the favour of God I have kept the faith.' He never lost a sense of thankfulness to the Lord for what he often referred to as 'the Gift of God.'

Interestingly, he never showed any bitterness towards the Lord with regard to his capture and subsequent slavery in Ireland, believing as he did that the Almighty had permitted this disaster to bring him to trust in Christ.

As his 'faith began to grow' one immediate result for this new born believer was an urge to pray. He records that he lifted his heart to God while at his work 'out in the woods' or 'on the mountainside' as many as 'one hundred times a day...' He would rise before dawn for prayer '...in snow and frost and rain, and felt no ill effect.' Again, looking back, he attributes his health and energy at that time to the fact that the Spirit was 'glowing' in him.

What days those must have been! He had had an encounter with the one who was '...sent to proclaim freedom for the prisoners and to release the oppressed.' (Gospel of Luke Chapter 4). Patrick was still a slave to men but his soul was free in God!

Who would true valour see
Let him come hither;
One here will constant be
Come wind come weather;
There's no discouragement
Shall make him once relent
His first avowed intent
To be a pilgrim.

John Bunyan.

During the night Paul had a vision of a
man of Macedonia ...begging him,
'come over to Macedonia and help us'
...we got ready at once to leave for
Macedonia concluding that God had
called us to preach the gospel to them
(Acts 16: 9, 10)

chapter four

Back in Britain

n the days immediately following his
conversion no divine deliverer arrived to restore
Patrick to his friends, but after six years in
captivity a voice in a dream one night told him
that he would soon return to his own country and, again,
shortly after, that a ship was ready for him. These were the
first of a number of similar revelations he tells us about,
each of which appeared to mark a turning point or crisis
experience in his career. He never doubted, nor have we
reason to disbelieve, that the 'messages' were from God to
give him encouragement and direction.

So he deserted his master and travelled two hundred
miles across the country, presumably on foot. A slave on
the run would have been exposed to considerable dangers
and hardship but Patrick gives us few details saying only
that he journeyed without fear and that the Lord guided
him. He found a ship ready to sail but his request for

passage was vigorously rejected. However as he turned away, praying as he walked, the men changed their mind - - soon he was saying farewell to Ireland! It has been debated as to whether the pagan sailors were traders or *raiders* but, in any case, there is evidence that they soon came to respect their visitor's bold witness for his faith and his confident prayers to God. After three days at sea they landed - exactly where has never been determined. While still in the company of these men, Patrick had more daunting hazards to overcome but eventually he made it back to his parents and relatives in Britain.

He had been torn ruthlessly away from the security of home and the care and love of his family. For six years he was denied all those things which we would regard as vital for any real quality of life, but speaking of that period he could later testify that the Lord 'guarded me and comforted me as would a father his son.' *Those years spent in communion with God and in isolation from friends gave Patrick a preparation for his future work that no theological seminary could match.* Even as a slave his manner of living made a profound impression on those who knew him and it is reasonable to assume that during that time he had opportunity to learn the Irish language and gain a knowledge of Irish culture. But now all that was behind him. He was free! As his friends and loved ones rejoiced with him it takes little effort to imagine his relief and satisfaction. Soon though he was to learn that his association with Ireland had not ended -- *it was only beginning.*

One night he had a vision in which he saw a man called Victoricus coming to him with a great number of letters. He read the title of one which said: 'THE CRY OF THE IRISH' and at that moment he seemed to hear the voice of the people who lived by the Wood of Voclut which is by the Western sea. Unitedly they said 'Holy youth we are asking you to come and walk among us again.' Patrick was so moved that he could read no more. A return to Ireland was hardly in his plans *but this changed everything.* It would seem that from that moment there was born in his heart a burden to bring the Gospel to that nation from which he says, pointedly, 'I was only just able to escape.'

Of interest is the mention of the 'Wood of Voclut' the only Irish place name found in any of his writings. This area has been fairly positively identified as being in the northern part of Co. Mayo not far from the present-day town of Killala. The fact that those who lived there are pictured as remembering Patrick's godly life and pleading that he would walk *again* among them, suggests very strongly that Ireland's patron saint spent the years of his captivity near the West coast of the island and *not* at Slemish in Co. Antrim. A westerly location would also explain why he had to travel two hundred miles to get a ship sailing for Britain. He does mention being subjected to other, shorter, periods of captivity and slavery during his mission. It is not impossible that one of these periods was spent in the Slemish area, thus giving rise to the popular tradition.

Patrick's 'call' was soon confirmed in other ways but now some years of preparation were required. He became a deacon in the local church and, eventually, was appointed a Bishop (or overseer) -- typically he remarks '...I was not worthy.' Some friends pleaded with tears and offered gifts to persuade him to call off his mission to Ireland but he refused to be moved. Again, typically, he says '...no thanks to me, it was God who prevailed in me.' Motivated by 'the love of Christ' he believed that the gift he had already received 'of knowing and loving God' was on condition that he leave, *for good*, his own 'country and kinsfolk.'

chapter five

Ireland Again!

reland in ancient times was regarded by the Roman world as 'the ends of the earth.' It was inhabited mainly by barbaric tribespeople, many of whom were of Celtic origin; they spoke in a tongue out of which has grown the present day Irish language. Though regarded as a primitive nation, the Irish were acknowledged as being competent sailors having seaworthy craft and were quite capable of piratical raids on Britain like the one described earlier. No towns had been built; no structured form of central government existed. The tribal unit, *the tuath*, was in reality a small kingdom consisting mainly of the extended family. The remains of the ring-forts *(raths)* which mark sites of population can still be seen in many places but the buildings themselves, not being constructed of enduring materials, have long since disappeared. Much of the country in the early fifth century was covered by forest and, in the absence of proper roads, some parts would have been inaccessible and desolate. The inhabitants of such areas would probably have regarded aliens with suspicion or even hostility.

This was the land to which Patrick returned as a missionary Bishop somewhere around the year 435 AD. He had with him his Latin Bible (or part of it), some form of financial support, the backing of a few Christians and, humanly speaking, very little else. Although always maintaining a Roman identity he determined never to leave Ireland. It became his adopted country and for some thirty years he spread a simple gospel far and wide, reaching even the tribes in isolated places.

He never claimed to be the first Christian to come to the island: there is reasonable evidence to suggest that Christianity first took root in southern parts and that Patrick worked mainly in the north. It is clear that he regarded himself as a pioneer evangelist and nowhere does he suggest that he was building on a foundation laid by earlier missionaries. That he came at all was a marvel even to himself. 'Who compelled me?' he asks and then gives the credit to the Spirit of God -- '...it was not my doing, this holy compassion that I have towards that nation which once took me captive and dealt havoc among the men and women servants of my father's house.'

A feature of the land through which he now travelled was the *absence of any snakes* but it was only after the space of several hundred years that somebody decided to give Patrick the credit for that! In the same vein there is plenty of evidence that he taught the doctrine of the Trinity, but did he use the shamrock to help his hearers grasp this truth?

-- It's possible, but uncertain.

He had none of the trappings of modern evangelism and often the roof of his meeting house would have been the sky above. Even the distribution of literature would have been pointless, for the tribespeople could not read: *It was left to them to judge the truth of the message by what they heard and by the character of the preacher.*

Patrick knew nothing of the great American continents, so, in the process of time, when he looked across the waters of the Atlantic he believed that Christ's commission to go into all the world had been carried out -- he had preached the gospel 'as far as the point where there is no one beyond.'

His Irish converts were never far from his heart; he rejoiced as he saw in them the fulfilment of the word of Jesus who predicted that many would come 'from the East and *from the West.'*

chapter six

Pacrick's Writings

trangely enough it would appear that for century after century there was little interest in the two works of Patrick already mentioned. Copies, which were entombed in various libraries and centres of learning across Europe, were seldom studied or even read. But in his wildest dreams Patrick could never have imagined the interest his stumbling words would create in the 20th century. His writings are what is termed 'primary source material' and are now recognised to be of paramount importance. For real history we require literature and Ireland *has* ancient literature -- Patrick's!

He is, as one writer has said, 'a lone voice from the silence of the fifth century in Britain and Ireland,' * and in view of this every detail of the two documents has been examined in numerous books and countless lectures. Can we be sure these writings are genuine? It is the virtually unanimous verdict of scholars that we can -- and this in

---

Liam de Paor --- Saint Patrick's World -- 1993

spite of the most critical investigations. Their undoubted early origin and subsequent history are impressive. More convincing still is the internal evidence: any reference in the text to coins, customs, and to social, religious, or political thought are in harmony with what is known of life and conditions pertaining in the twilight days of the Roman Empire. Additionally, these records are so individual in tone that the reader is convinced that a forgery is out of the question and that the words of both are indeed the testimony of one man -- an evangelical missionary in Ireland!

Of the two writings of St. Patrick the 'Letter' is by far the shorter. It was sent to Coroticus who was probably one of a number of petty rulers who had taken power after the decline of Roman influence in Britain. This man with his soldiers had attacked a group of recently baptized believers: some of these Irish Christians had been killed and others were carried off to be sold into slavery. Patrick doesn't mince his words. He denounces this atrocity, pleads for the release of the captives and warns that those responsible are heading for punishment in hell unless they repent. He accuses these men of selling women to heathens for wretched temporal gain and quotes the words of Jesus in the book of Matthew, 'What good will it be for a man if he gains the whole world and yet loses his own soul.'

It is obvious that Patrick was deeply distressed by this cruel blow inflicted on the infant Church. Almost in despair he cries out 'O most beautiful and most beloved brothers and children whom I have begotten in Christ, what am I to do for you?' His one consolation was complete confidence that those killed had departed this life to their reward in Heaven.

He refers to the raiders as 'murderers' and 'sons of the Devil' but his confidence in the power of the gospel is so strong that he holds out even to them, the possibility of repentance and forgiveness.

The other undoubted work of Patrick, his 'Confession', was so named by himself in the very last line 'this is my confession before I die.' It is to this document that we are indebted for most of the precious information we possess concerning his life and work. Some writers now give it the more meaningful title of 'Patrick's Declaration' for it was not to any great degree a confession of sin but rather a record of God's dealing with him and a statement of his faith. It was written near the end of his career, perhaps in semi-retirement, and, as the Irish language existed then only in spoken form, he employed Latin.

Patrick was a captive in Ireland when he should have been receiving further education; consequently he was unable to write in what can be called the literary or classical Latin of the scholars. His was colloquial Latin; the sort he had picked up in his early schooling, the language of the street and the marketplace. He was sensitive, excessively sensitive, about his lack of learning, but, in a strange way, the thing he regretted so much has worked out for our good -- there is no fancy padding in his speech -- no need for us to plough through the flowery rhetoric that seemed to plague much of the literature of the Roman world. Patrick, as we say in Ireland, called a spade a spade! To become familiar with his faltering and sometimes ungrammatical writings can be a moving experience, for in them we meet a man with remarkable faith, *a singularly humble and godly man.* As we read, Patrick *compels* us to believe him. Some historians who would not be entirely in sympathy with his fervent Christian convictions are so impressed with his childlike sincerity that even they *find it unthinkable that he should deceive.*

How we would have loved that Patrick had provided us with much more historical information about pre-Christian Ireland than he did; but then that was not the reason why he wrote. He wrote to glorify God. His writings were about spiritual matters. In this respect a further guarantee about the reliability of his writings is the standards the author imposed upon himself -- they were composed, he says, in the knowledge that one day he would stand in judgment for any false or idle words that he might use.

Again in a strange way it makes the whole thing all the more real and intriguing when we see that it was never Patrick's intention to provide information for future generations; writing did not come easily to him -- he only put pen to paper because events demanded it.

The 'Letter' was an outcry against distressing violence and bloodshed. The 'Confession' was a response to betrayal and false accusation. It is not too much to say that, had it not been for these dark periods in his experience we might not possess today these priceless treasures in which we have the privilege of looking at real situations and at the thoughts and reactions of a very real person.

God moves in a mysterious way
His wonders to perform;
He plants His footprints in the sea
And rides upon the storm.

- Cowper

Yellow Flags, Co. Clare

About twelve early manuscripts of the "Confession" still exist. The oldest is that which was beautifully written in the "Book of Armagh" in the year 807 AD by a famous scribe called Ferndomnagh.

Part of a page from that book is reproduced opposite by permission of THE BOARD OF TRINITY COLLEGE, DUBLIN.

The opening words of the Confession on the ninth line can easily be identified ~ "Ego Patricius peccator,..." I am Patrick a sinner....

chapter seven

Patrick's Faith

he foundation of Patrick's faith was the Bible. *He was a man of one book.* Its words were his complete and sole authority and gave him inspiration for this life and confidence as to the next! His brief writings contain a multitude of scripture quotations; nearly two hundred can be identified: These he uses to describe his experiences, to convey his feelings, and to justify his mission. There is perhaps an assumption that many of his readers would be familiar with the sacred book. He was not, nor would he have claimed to be, among the greatest Biblical scholars. Parts of the Bible gave him difficulties but none gave him doubts -- he was the sort of person who took God at his word and found that it worked.

The only place where Patrick quotes from a source other than the Bible is near the beginning of the 'Confession' where he sets out a compact scriptural statement of belief. This creed, certainly not his own composition, was very probably one that had been adopted by the British Church and thus is of considerable historical interest. Here is a part of it:

'...every tongue should confess... that Jesus Christ is Lord and God; and we believe in Him and await His coming which will happen soon, as judge of the living and the dead. ...The Holy Spirit... makes those who believe and obey to be the sons of God and co-heirs with Christ and we confess and adore Him, one God in the Trinity of sacred name.'

Patrick's interpretation of some scripture passages is questionable and we might not agree with all of his ideas but as Dr. Hanson has said, 'he goes straight to the heart of the biblical message, to the promises of God in the Old Testament, the redemption brought by Christ in the New.' His own salvation had come about by the grace of God alone and in the absence of human help so he was committed to preaching the good news of God's free gift of salvation to all who would repent and believe. He recognised that true believers were reborn in God and that such should be baptized.

He taught the resurrection of the body and *emphasised the return of Christ*. He also had a deep conviction regarding a coming day of judgment from which said he, '...no one will be able to escape.' It goes without saying that he was a man of prayer and one who never separated his doctrine from his lifestyle and mission. To him Christians were a 'letter of Christ' and he said, in effect, I cannot keep silent, *I want to tell the world about His goodness and grace.*

Patrick had a faith, not born or developed in the study, but forged on the anvil of hardship and disaster and tested by pain and disappointment. Some students of Patrick have remarked on the resemblance between him and the Apostle Paul. As Paul faced the executioner at Rome he used words that would fit well the character of Ireland's apostle as he too came near the end of his life -- 'I have fought a good fight, I have finished my course, I have kept the faith. Henceforth there is laid up for me a crown of righteousness...'

If Christ be God and died for me
then no sacrifice can be too great
for me to make for Him.
C. T. Studd.

chapter eight

Patrick's Mission

Returning one time from a visit to England I stood on the deck of the ship and as the outline of the coast of Ireland began to take shape through the mist, I pondered as to what thoughts must have been in Patrick's heart as he made a similar crossing many centuries ago. Whatever emotions crowded his mind, of this we can be sure, he had no regrets -- *he was a man with one purpose and one mission.*

He lived in momentous days; theological conflicts swept across Europe, the great Roman Empire was in serious trouble, Rome itself had been overrun by the Goths in 410 AD -- Patrick makes no mention of any of it! 'I exist,' he says, 'to teach tribes for my God ..... I am a slave in Christ to an outlandish nation because of the unspeakable glory of eternal life which is in Christ Jesus our Lord.'

His return to preach the Gospel in the land where he once was a slave gave him what was surely one of the most daunting and frightening tasks in the history of Christian missions. There is no reason to suppose that any helpers came with him and in fact there were those in Britain who thought the venture was madness and would come to an abrupt and bloody end.

The measure of the opposition from pagan tribes cannot be fully known but it was sullen and menacing. Patrick speaks of 'insults' and 'many persecutions.' On his travels he was robbed, 'thrown into chains' and even confined to periods of slavery. There were many occasions when he says that *his very life was in danger*, but he had a commitment to cope with all this. 'I am prepared to give my life without hesitation and most gladly for His name and it is there (in Ireland) that I wish to spend it until I die...' *It seems he never even considered the possibility of quitting!*

On top of the physical hazards there came an even more distressing development; an attempt was made in Britain to discredit both him and his work. 'I was attacked' he said, 'I was violently pushed to make me fall.' He was rejected by some men in high position and was betrayed by one whom he regarded as 'his closest friend.' In all this Patrick never recorded any bitterness but only love and forgiveness.

In a particularly touching passage he recounts that at the time of his trial the Lord drew especially close to him in a night-time experience saying as it were, 'whoever touches you touches the apple of my eye.' (From words in the book of Zechariah.) He rejoiced greatly that the outcome of the affair was not disaster but rather a confirmation of his mission and he records that from that time on he felt a *great sense of power within him.*

Who were those men of high position in the Church who found fault with Patrick's mission and sat in judgment upon him? *The spade of time has buried their names beyond recall.* What if Patrick had turned away from the call of the Irish and decided not to waste his life in a pagan land? *His name too would be gone forever!*

Even after many years in Ireland 'assassination', 'treachery', 'reduction to slavery' or 'some accident' were daily possibilities. Patrick's response to these threats was one that disarmed their terror, and nowhere is his faith and strength better demonstrated than in these memorable words, *'I fear none of these things on account of the promises of heaven because I have thrown myself into the hands of Almighty God who reigns everywhere.'* He appears like a bare-footed child walking in a minefield. We marvel that he is not destroyed! A closer look reveals the arm of Christ around him, taking him through. Patrick knew and was happy to accept the fact that those who put their trust in God are not promised an easy journey *but only a safe arrival!*

Rejoice in the Lord always.
I will say it again: Rejoice!
St. Paul

chapter nine

Patrick's Praise

t has already been suggested that Patrick composed the 'Confession' as a reply to those who had ridiculed him. Another and altogether more obvious reason was to give thanks and praise to his Heavenly Father for all the benefits he had received from Him.

Sometimes he confuses his readers by jumping abruptly from one subject to another, but one can hardly fail to notice that dominant in nearly every part of his writings is *a note of praise and confidence.* His whole spirit is one of thankfulness for the gift of salvation, of being in debt to God for all his mercies. '...I give unwearying thanks to my God' he says, and in another place 'God has shown that I should believe on Him *endlessly as trustworthy.*' This attitude to the Lord didn't change with the circumstances and he could say 'I exalt and glorify your name wherever I happen to be not only when things go well but also in troubles!' *Patrick had the joy of being thankful*. He seems to have captured a song of praise in his heart and a joy in Christ that were beyond the reach of even the harshest and most unfair treatment that man could inflict upon him.

Another clue as to why Patrick majored on praise was his sense of wonder and gratitude (and almost unbelief!) that *the Lord had chosen him*. In the struggles and hardships of his work he was sustained by the confidence that he was in God's hands. He never seemed to lose sight of the fact that he was simply the human instrument of Christ's bid for the hearts of Irish people. His words were these '...I commend my soul to my most trustworthy God on whose behalf I am carrying out a mission...' As a consequence of that there was no possibility of failure, for, having given everything to God, what had he to lose?

Additionally, Patrick's optimism and cheerfulness sprung from the fact that he lived with eternal values in view -- having settled the future of his soul the grave held no fears. Some pagans worshipped the sun in the sky but near the end of the 'Confession' he claimed '...We who believe in and adore the true sun Christ who will never die nor will anyone die who has done his will.' Contemplating the possibility of a martyr's death and of his corpse being torn to pieces by dogs or wild animals he had this to say '...I believe confidently that if this were to happen to me I have gained my soul along with my body because *without a shadow of a doubt* on that day we shall rise in the radiance of the sun ...in the glory of Christ Jesus our Redeemer as children of the living God and co-heirs with Christ...'

In our generation communism, among other ideologies, has tried to build a utopian society based on man's ability to succeed without God. The failure of this concept as seen in parts of Eastern Europe needs no comment. But neither has capitalism nor materialism in themselves been able to fully satisfy the basic needs of mankind. Television serves up its endless helpings of comedy, culture, and entertainment; in many countries people have more money, more travel opportunities, more leisure than ever before but 'The Samaritans' are not redundant -- the problem of empty hearts has not gone away.

Patrick says that prior to his conversion he 'had deserted God' but then he found that Jesus could satisfy his inner being, and in later years discovered such joy and fulfillment in life that he would not have exchanged his missionary labours and the companionship of his converts in Ireland for the palace of a king.

To heaven the place of His abode
He brings my weary feet;
Shows me the Glories of my God
And makes my joy complete.
S. Stennett

chapter ten

Patrick's Legacy

 his book has not been written to glorify Patrick. If what has been said up to this point conveys the idea that he was faultless or that he was some kind of superman then we need to pause to correct that impression. *He was not perfect.* It would diminish the value of his memory to suggest that he was. On his own admission he made many blunders and the prominent people of his day would probably have regarded him as being a very ordinary man.

There appears to have been little enthusiasm anywhere for his crusade. He came to Ireland as an outsider, a foreigner, and, as such, completely vulnerable -- no laws existed in Irish tribal society to protect him. All the odds were against the success of a Christian mission but this ordinary man saw extraordinary things happen!

How did Patrick go about his work of evangelism? He gives us few details. It would be tedious, he tells us, to give an account of all his labours, and he goes on to say that he does not want to bore his readers. We can't help wishing that he had not worried about boring his readers! If only he had taken us with him and given us a pen picture of what it was like to make the first contacts with tribespeople who had never before heard the gospel. There is certainly no hint in his writings that he could depend on the help of an angel when things got rough. *He never claimed that he could perform miracles or that churches were founded nearly everywhere he went.* All we have is a simple reference to -- '...the children of God whom he has gathered at the ends of the earth through my exhortation' and a mention of '...the flock of the Lord increasing in Ireland as the result of hard work.'

What was achieved by Patrick's exhortation and hard work? Well, the full story is known only to Heaven and we will have to wait for the details, but of this we can be sure -- in *his* lifetime *Ireland was not won for Christ.* It would seem from what records are available that when Patrick died the land was still largely pagan and opposed to Christianity. But, as he claims in a number of places, thousands of men and women did believe and were baptized. Incredibly, he did see the spiritual structures of the Christian Church gradually take shape and a visible community of believers begin to influence a land where, up to that time, spiritual darkness had reigned almost unhindered.

The 'Confession' records it beautifully by saying that it had happened that people who never had a knowledge of God, and who had worshipped only idols and filthy things, were now a people of the Lord and called the sons of God.

How these Celtic people could have been persuaded to turn away from belief in magic and from the gods of their druidic tradition is, to some, a complete mystery, especially since it is plain that the choice the converts had made was not an easy one. Some had to endure 'persecutions and false accusations.' Patrick commends the believers from the slave population that '...they hold out steadfastly against intimidation and threats.' It is not unlikely that some Christians were martyred.

From our position in history any explanation of Patrick's success is, of course, inadequate, but motivated by the love of Christ his message would have been simple, warm, direct, and based on the Holy Scriptures of which he was so familiar. We can readily accept that he was a man under the direction of God and that his preaching, like that of St. Paul's, was '...not with wise and persuasive words but with a demonstration of the Spirit's power.' (1 Cor. 2:4) Even pagan tribes must have been awed by the holiness and absolute sincerity of his life. *His God was real.* Touched by the strange power of love and of the gospel many ventured their life into the hands of this Jesus that Patrick talked about -- and having done so they were not disappointed.

Sent by Christ, committed to his mission for the rest of his life, he was not the only one to spread the good news, but there is little doubt that his labours greatly influenced the development of a vibrant, independent Celtic church; the beginning of a movement that would see men like Columba leave for other shores to hold aloft the torch of truth in a growing darkness: A movement that would produce the great monasteries where piety and learning would flourish and cause Ireland to be known as a *'land of saints and scholars.'*

It is just like Patrick that at the end of the 'Confession' he implores those who read it not to give him the credit for what was achieved, '...but you are to think and it must be sincerely believed that it was the gift of God.'

In the immediate centuries after his death there was little or no mention of him in any of the world's literature and it seems that the knowledge of his work, handed down by word of mouth, all but faded away. But in the mercy and plan of God his writings survived in the darkness of the fifth and sixth centuries and in due time these writings were to bring to life again the character and career of a humble and truly remarkable man. The legendary story of Patrick lighting the Paschal fire at Tara in defiance of the High King is only a story but he *did* light a flame in Ireland -- *one that has never gone out.*

chapter eleven

Patrick's Treasure

id Patrick ever consider marriage? Well that's a question you would have to ask him yourself! He did on one occasion refer to a 'beautiful Irish woman' but it was certainly not in any romantic context. My own guess is that in the circumstances of his mission he would have put aside any such thoughts. In harmony with some words of Paul found in the New Testament, Patrick might have considered that for him to marry would be good but not to marry better.

There was, however, a great love affair in his life, one that neither cruel experiences nor passing years ever caused to grow cold; it was that love and devotion he had for Jesus Christ. Some words translated from a very old Irish hymn could well have been his --

Riches I need not nor man's empty praise
Thou mine inheritance now and always:
Thou and thou only, first in my heart
High King of Heaven my treasure thou art.

A slab of granite in the precincts of Down Cathedral bears, in Irish letters, the inscription 'PATRICK,' but the passing centuries have removed any evidence that would tell us where the aged saint was actually buried. Perhaps even in this we can see the wise hand of providence, for we can think of Patrick belonging, not just to some hallowed corner, but to all parts of that island where centuries ago he brought the light of the gospel.

Because of his uncompromising stand against evil and pagan forces a violent end to his crusade must never have seemed far away, but *in coming to terms with death he found the secret of living.* He referred to himself as 'a sinner,' 'poorly educated,' and 'unsatisfactory,' but he was God's man for Ireland and is, even today, a symbol of Christian courage and a testimony to the unfailing love of Christ.

In his book 'Who was Saint Patrick?' E. A. Thompson considers the hopelessness of having any real knowledge of Patrick if by some 'hideous mischance' his writings had been lost. *But no such hideous mischance occurred.* Many would believe that the survival of the documents is not the result of 'good luck' or 'an accident' as some have suggested, but rather that their availability today is the seal of God's approval on the life and ministry of this humble man.

When Patrick expressed a desire that by his writing people would get to know what he was like, he achieved that aim in a way far beyond what he could have imagined, for as one Irish journalist has said, 'the man comes alive in his halting but moving prose.'* It is not hard for those with similar convictions and missionary vision to discover in these records a kindred spirit and in a very real sense to come to know the real St. Patrick. Some of his text may be obscure and his reasoning at times hard to follow, but nothing, *absolutely nothing, can dim the excitement of the fact that here, written in Ireland, are the very words of a Christian believer of the early centuries of the Church.*

Neither of the two main traditions in Ireland can justly lay exclusive claim to St. Patrick; *he transcends any such divisions.* But can his life and words offer any ray of hope, not only to the people of one small island, but to other divided communities? Well, it's common knowledge that situations are changed when people are changed. The challenge of Patrick comes to us as individuals; not with regard to a formal loyalty to a particular religion, but as to our personal relationship with Jesus. Patrick's own experience calls us to repentance and illustrates *the joyful possibility of a new birth into God's family and into a living faith in a living Christ.*

I think again of a teenage slave finding such reality in God that the lonely woods and hillsides of Co. Mayo became to him a cathedral of prayer and praise. As a Christian I am profoundly challenged by his response, in later years, to the call of the Irish so vividly brought to him in a night vision. What could have moved him to turn away from the prosperity and comfort he could have enjoyed in

Alannah Hopkin -- 'The Living Legend of St. Patrick' 1990

Britain? What made him turn his back on worldly position and make his home for the rest of his life in that land which had dealt so cruelly with him? *To Patrick it was reason enough that it was what Jesus wanted him to do.*

We have no idea of what Patrick looked like and little idea of what he wore, but we do have *his very own words* -- providing for us a window into his soul and giving us a legacy of faith and inspiration for our generation.

• • •

In the final analysis, however, the two writings which were born at the dawn of Ireland's Christianity and have survived the ravages of time, do more than supply us with information on Saint Patrick. They cause us to reflect on the loving purposes of Almighty God. *They point beyond the human evangelist to the unchanging majesty of One whose coming has divided the chronicles of history and whose death and resurrection have opened up a way of life for the people of every nation.* I'm sure that's the way Patrick would have wanted it to be.

Translations of Patrick's Writings

~ EXPLANATORY NOTE ~

In 404 AD the scholar Jerome completed his famous Vulgate edition of the Scriptures, a version that was gradually accepted for use by Christians throughout much of the world. The Bible Patrick used was an earlier one sometimes referred to as the OLD LATIN version, one of a number of translations which existed prior to the work of Jerome. This fact lends support to the placing of Patrick's early life at the end of the 4th century but it does cause problems with his Scripture quotations. The old version, which appeared to include the Apocrypha, had deficiencies, and readers may notice that these quotations (some of which may have been written from memory) differ somewhat from the text of the Bible with which they are familiar.

I want to record that a debt of gratitude is owed to the scholars whose research in recent years has provided a greater knowledge and deeper appreciation of the kind of Latin that Patrick used. Even with the benefits of this valuable work, putting the two writings into modern English is still not a straightforward task; the translator has to recognise the possibility of some corruption of the text by early copyists, and has to struggle at times with determining and expressing what the writer actually intended to say.

To grasp the spirit of the 'Confession' and 'Letter', to sense the situation in which they were written, and to get near to the heart of Patrick himself, may require several thoughtful readings and some study. *It is worth the effort.*

The following translations, first published in 1953 are by the late Ludwig Bieler of Dublin, an eminent authority on Patrick's writings.

Croagh Patrick

The woodlands in early summer

The Confession of St. Patrick

am Patrick, a sinner, most unlearned, the least of all the faithful, and utterly despised by many. My father was Calpornius, a deacon, son of Potitus, a priest, of the village Bannavem Taburniae; he had a country seat nearby, and there I was taken captive.

I was then about sixteen years of age. I did not know the true God. I was taken into captivity to Ireland with many thousands of people - and deservedly so, because we turned away from God, and did not keep His commandments, and did not obey our priests, who used to remind us of our salvation. And the Lord *brought over us the wrath of his anger and scattered us among many nations,* even unto the utmost part of the earth, where now my littleness is placed among strangers.

And there *the Lord opened the sense of my unbelief* that I might at last remember my sins and *be converted with all my heart to the Lord my God*, who had regard for my abjection, and mercy on my youth and ignorance, and watched over me before I knew Him, and before I was able to distinguish between good and evil, and guarded me, and comforted me as would a father his son.

Hence I cannot be silent - nor, indeed, is it expedient - about the great benefits and the great grace which the Lord has deigned to bestow upon me in the land of my captivity; for this we can give to God in return after having been chastened by Him, to exalt and praise His wonders before every nation that is anywhere under the heaven.

Because there is no other God, nor ever was, nor will be, than God the Father unbegotten, without beginning, from whom is all beginning, the Lord of the universe, as we have been taught; and His son Jesus Christ, whom we declare to have always been with the Father, spiritually and ineffably begotten by the Father before the beginning of the world, before all beginning; and by Him are made all things visible and invisible. He was made man, and, having defeated death, was received into heaven by the Father; *and He hath given Him all power over all names in heaven, on earth, and under the earth, and every tongue shall confess to Him that Jesus Christ is Lord and God,* in whom we believe, and whose advent we expect soon to be, judge of the living and of the dead, who will render to everyman according to his deeds; and *He has poured forth upon us abundantly the Holy Spirit,* the gift and pledge of immortality, who makes those who believe and obey sons of God and joint heirs with

Christ; and Him do we confess and adore, one God in the Trinity of the Holy Name.

For He Himself has said through the Prophet; *Call upon me in the day of thy trouble, and I will deliver thee, and thou shalt glorify me. And again He says; it is honourable to reveal and confess the works of God.*

Although I am imperfect in many things, I nevertheless wish that my brethren and kinsmen should know what sort of person I am, so that they may understand my heart's desire.

I know well the testimony of my Lord, who in the Psalm declares: *Thou wilt destroy them that speak a lie. And again He says: The mouth that belieth killeth the soul.* And the same Lord says in the Gospel: *Every idle word that men shall speak, they shall render an account for it on the day of judgment.*

And so I should dread exceedingly, with fear and trembling, this sentence on that day when no one will be able to escape or hide, but we all, without exception, shall have to give an account even of our smallest sins before the judgment seat of the Lord Christ.

For this reason I long had in mind to write, but hesitated until now; I was afraid of exposing myself to the talk of men, because I have not studied like the others, who thoroughly imbibed law and Sacred Scripture, and never had to change from the language of their childhood days, but were able to make it still more perfect. In our case, what I had to say had to be translated into a tongue foreign to me, as can be easily proved from the savour of my writing, which betrays how little instruction and training I have had in the art of words; for, so says Scripture, *by the tongue will be discovered the wise man, and understanding, and knowledge, and the teaching of truth.*

But of what help is an excuse, however true, especially if combined with presumption, since now, in my old age, I strive for something that I did not acquire in youth? It was my sins that prevented me from fixing in my mind what before I had barely read through. But who believes me, though I should repeat what I started out with?

As a youth, nay, almost as a boy not able to speak, I was taken captive, before I knew what to pursue and what to avoid. Hence today I blush and fear exceedingly to reveal my lack of education; for I am unable to tell my story to those versed in the art of concise writing - in such a way, I mean, as my spirit and mind long to do, and so that the sense of my words expresses what I feel.

But if indeed it had been given to me as it was given to others, then I would not be silent because of my desire of thanksgiving; and if perhaps some people think me arrogant for doing so in spite of my lack of knowledge and my slow tongue, it is, after all, written; *The stammering tongues shall quickly learn to speak peace.*

How much more should we earnestly strive to do this, we, who are, so Scripture says, *a letter of Christ for salvation unto the utmost part of the earth,* and, though not an eloquent one, yet... *written in your hearts, not with ink, but with the spirit of the living God!* And again the Spirit witnesses that even rusticity was created by the Highest.

Whence I, once rustic, exiled, unlearned, who does not know how to provide for the future, this at least I know most certainly that before I was humiliated I was like a stone lying in the deep mire; and He that is mighty came and in His mercy lifted me up, and raised me aloft, and placed me on the top of the wall. And therefore I ought to cry out aloud and so also render something to the Lord for His great benefits here and in eternity - benefits which the mind of men is unable to appraise.

Wherefore, then, be astonished, ye great and little that fear God, and you men of letters on your estates, listen and pore over this. Who was it that roused up me, the fool that I am, from the midst of those who in the eyes of men are wise, and expert in law, and powerful in word and in everything? And He inspired me - me, the outcast of this world - before others, to be the man (if only I could!) who, with fear and reverence and without blame, should faithfully serve the people to whom the love of Christ conveyed and gave me for the duration of my life, if I should be worthy; yes indeed, to serve them humbly and sincerely.

In the light, therefore, of our faith in the Trinity I must make this choice, regardless of danger I must make known the gift of God and everlasting consolation, without fear and frankly I must spread everywhere the name of God so that after my decease I may leave a bequest to my brethren and sons whom I have baptized in the Lord - so many thousands of people.

And I was not worthy, nor was I such that the Lord should grant this to His servant; that after my misfortunes and so great difficulties, after my captivity, after the lapse of so many years, He should give me so great a grace in behalf of that nation - a thing which once, in my youth, I never expected nor thought of.

But after I came to Ireland - every day I had to tend sheep, and many times a day I prayed - the love of God and His fear came to me more and more, and my faith was strengthened. And my spirit was moved so that in a single day I would say as many as a hundred prayers, and almost as many in the night, and this even when I was staying in the woods and on the mountains; and I used to get up for prayer before daylight, through snow, through frost, through rain, and I felt no harm, and there was no sloth in me - as I now see, because the spirit within me was then fervent.

And there one night I heard in my sleep a voice saying to me: 'It is well that you fast, soon you will go to your own country.' And, again, after a short while, I heard a voice saying to me: 'See, your ship is ready.' And it was not near, but at a distance of perhaps two hundred miles, and I had never been there, nor did I know a living soul there; and then I took to flight, and I left the man with whom I had stayed for six years. And I went in the strength of God who directed my way to my good, and I feared nothing until I came to that ship.

And the day that I arrived the ship was set afloat, and I said that I was able to pay for my passage with them. But the captain was not pleased, and with indignation he answered harshly; 'It is of no use for you to ask us to go along with us.' And when I heard this, I left them in order to return to the hut where I was staying. And as I went, I began to pray; and before I had ended my prayer, I heard one of them shouting behind me: 'Come, hurry, we shall take you on in good faith; make friends with us in whatever way you like.' And so on that day I refused to suck their breasts for fear of God, but rather hoped they would come to the faith of Jesus Christ, because they were pagans. And thus I had my way with them, and we set sail at once.

And after three days we reached land, and for twenty-eight days we travelled through deserted country. And they lacked food, and hunger overcame them; and the next day the captain said to me: 'Tell me, Christian: you say that your God is great and all-powerful; why, then, do you not pray for us? As you can see, we are suffering from hunger; it is unlikely indeed that we shall ever see a human being again.'

I said to them full of confidence: 'Be truly converted with all your heart to the Lord my God, because nothing is impossible for Him, that this day He may send you food on your way until you be satisfied; for He has abundance everywhere.' And, with the help of God, so it came to pass: suddenly a herd of pigs appeared on the road before our eyes, and they killed many of them; and there they stopped for two nights and fully recovered their strength, and their hounds received their fill, for many of them had grown weak and were half-dead along the way. And from that day they had plenty of food. They also found wild honey, and offered some of it to me, and one of them said: 'This we offer in sacrifice.' Thanks be to God, I tasted none of it.

That same night, when I was asleep, Satan assailed me violently, a thing I shall remember as long as I shall be in this body. And he fell upon me like a huge rock, and I could not stir a limb. But whence came it into my mind, ignorant as I am, to call upon Elias? And meanwhile I saw the sun rise in the sky, and while I was shouting 'Elias! Elias!' with all my might, suddenly the splendour of that sun fell on me and immediately freed me of all misery. And I believe that I was sustained by Christ my Lord, and that His Spirit was even then crying out on my behalf, and I hope it will be so on the day of my tribulation, as is written in the Gospel: On that day, the Lord declares, it is not you that speak, but the Spirit of your Father that speaketh in you.

And once again, after many years, I fell into captivity. On that first night I stayed with them. I heard a divine message saying to me: 'Two months will you be with them.' And so it came to pass: on the sixtieth night thereafter the Lord delivered me out of their hands.

Also on our way God gave us food and fire and dry weather every day, until, on the tenth day, we met people. As I said above, we travelled twenty-eight days through deserted country, and the night that we met people we had no food left.

And again after a few years I was in Britain with my people, who received me as their son, and sincerely besought me that now at last, having suffered so many hardships, I should not leave them and go elsewhere.

And there I saw in the night the vision of a man, whose name was Victoricus, coming as it were from Ireland, with countless letters. And he gave me one of them, and I read the opening words of the letter, which were: 'The voice of the Irish'; and as I read the beginning of the letter I thought that at the same moment I heard their voice - they were those beside the Wood of Voclut, which is near the Western Sea - and thus did they cry out as with one mouth: 'We ask thee, boy, come and walk among us once more.'

And I was quite broken in heart, and could read no further, and so I woke up. Thanks be to God, after many years the Lord gave to them according to their cry.

And another night - whether within me, or beside me, I know not, God knoweth - they called me most unmistakable with words which I heard but could not understand, except that at the end of the prayer He spoke thus: 'He that has laid down his life for thee, it is he that speaketh in thee'; and so I awoke full of joy.

And again I saw Him praying in me, and I was as it were within my body, and I heard Him above me, that is, over the inward man, and there He prayed mightily with groanings. And all the time I was astonished, and wondered, and thought with myself who it could be that prayed in me. But at the end of the prayer He spoke, saying that He was the Spirit; and so I woke up, and remembered the Apostle saying: *The Spirit helpeth the infirmities of our prayer. For we know not what we should pray for as we ought, but the Spirit Himself asketh for us with unspeakable groanings, which cannot be expressed in words; and again: The Lord our advocate asketh for us.*

And when I was attacked by a number of my seniors who came forth and brought up my sins against my laborious episcopate, on that day indeed was I struck so that I might have fallen now and for eternity; but the Lord graciously spared the stranger and sojourner for His name and came mightily to my help in this affliction. Verily, not slight was the shame and blame that fell upon me! I ask God that it may not be reckoned to them as sin.

As cause for proceeding against me they found - after thirty years! - a confession I had made before I was a deacon. In the anxiety of my troubled mind I confided to my dearest friend what I had done in my boyhood one day, nay, in one hour, because I was not yet strong. I know not, God knoweth - whether I was then fifteen years old; and I did not believe in the living God, nor did I so from my childhood, but lived in death and unbelief until I was severely chastised and really humiliated, by hunger and nakedness, and that daily.

On the other hand, I did not go to Ireland of my own accord, not until I had nearly perished; but this was rather for my good, for thus was I purged by the Lord; and He made me fit so that I might be now what was once far from me - that I should care and labour for the salvation of others whereas then I did not even care about myself.

On that day, then, when I was rejected by those referred to and mentioned above, in that night I saw a vision of the night. There was a writing without honour against my face, and at the same time I heard God's voice saying to me: 'We have seen with displeasure the face of Deisignatus' (thus revealing his name). He did not say: 'Thou hast seen,' but: 'We have seen,' as if He included Himself, as He says: *He who toucheth you toucheth as it were the apple of my eye.*

Therefore I give Him thanks who hath strengthened me in everything, as He did not frustrate the journey upon which I had decided, and the work which I had learned from Christ my Lord; but I rather felt after this no little strength, and my trust was proved right before God and men.

And so I say boldly, my conscience does not blame me now or in the future: God is my witness that I have not lied in the account which I have given you.

But the more am I sorry for my dearest friend that we had to hear what he said. To him I had confided my very soul! And I was told by some of the brethren before that defence - at which I was not present nor was I in Britain, nor was it suggested by me - that he would stand up for me in my absence. He had even said to me in person: 'Look, you should be raised to the rank of bishop!' - of which I was not worthy. But whence did it come to him afterwards that he let me down before all, good and evil, and publicly, in a matter in which he had favoured me before spontaneously and gladly - and not he alone, but the Lord, who is greater than all?

Enough of this. I must not, however, hide God's gift which He bestowed upon me in the land of my captivity; because then I earnestly sought Him, and there I found Him, and He saved me from all evil because - so I believe - of His Spirit that dwelleth in me. Again, boldly said. But God knows it, had this been said to me by a man, I had perhaps remained silent for the love of Christ.

Hence, then, I give unweaned thanks to God, who kept me faithful in the day of my temptation, so that today I can confidently offer Him my soul as a living sacrifice - to Christ my Lord, who saved me out of all my troubles. Thus I can say: 'Who am I, O Lord, and to what hast Thou called me, Thou who didst assist me with such divine power that today I constantly exalt and magnify Thy name among the heathens wherever I may be, and not only in good days but also in tribulations?'

So indeed I must accept with equanimity whatever befalls me, be it good or evil, and always give thanks to God, who taught me to trust in Him always without hesitation, and who must have heard my prayer so that I, however ignorant I was, in the last days I dared to undertake such a holy and wonderful work - thus imitating somehow those who, as the Lord once foretold, would preach His Gospel for a testimony to all nations before the end of the world. So we have seen it, and so it has been fulfilled: indeed, we are witnesses that the Gospel has been preached unto those parts beyond which there lives nobody.

Now, it would be tedious to give a detailed account of all my labours or even a part of them. Let me tell you briefly how the merciful God often freed me from slavery and from twelve dangers in which my life was at stake - not to mention numerous plots, which I cannot express in words; for I do not want to bore my readers. But God is my witness, who knows all things even before they come to pass, as He used to forewarn even me, poor wretch that I am, of many things by a divine message.

How came I by this wisdom, which was not in me, who neither knew the number of my days nor knew what God was? Whence was given to me afterwards the gift so great, so salutary - to know God and to love Him, although at the price of leaving my country and my parents?

And many gifts were offered to me in sorrow and tears, and I offended the donors, much against the wishes of some of my seniors; but, guided by God, in no way did I agree with them or acquiesce. It was not grace of my own, but God, who is strong in me and resists them all - as He had done when I came to the people of Ireland to preach the Gospel, and to suffer insult from the unbelievers, hearing the reproach of my going abroad, and many persecutions even unto bonds, and to give my free birth for the benefit of others; and, should I be worthy, I am prepared to give even my life without hesitation and most gladly for His name, and it is there that I wish to spend it until I die, if the Lord would grant it to me.

For I am very much God's debtor, who gave me such great grace that many people were reborn in God through me and afterwards confirmed, and that clerics were ordained for them everywhere, for a people just coming to the faith, whom the Lord took from the utmost parts of the earth, as He once had promised through His prophets: *To Thee the Gentiles shall come from the ends of the earth and shall say: 'How false are the idols that our fathers got for themselves, and there is no profit in them' - and again: I have set Thee as a light among the Gentiles, that Thou mayest be for salvation unto the utmost part of the earth.*

And there I wish to wait for His promise who surely never deceives, as He promises in the Gospel: *They shall come from the east and the west, and shall sit down with Abraham and Isaac and Jacob* - as we believe the faithful will come from all the world.

For that reason, therefore, we ought to fish well and diligently, as the Lord exhorts in advance and teaches, saying: *Come ye after me, and I will make you to be fishers of men.* And again He says through the prophets: *Behold, I send many fishes and hunters, saith God,* and so on. Hence it was most necessary to spread our nets so that a great multitude and throng might be caught for God, and that there be clerics everywhere to baptize and exhort a people in need and want, as the Lord in the Gospel states, exhorts and teaches, saying: *Going therefore now, teach ye all nations, baptizing them in the name of the Father, and the Son, and the Holy Spirit, teaching them to observe all things whatsoever I have commanded you: and behold I am with you all days even to the consummation of the world.* And again He says: *Go ye therefore into the whole world, and preach the Gospel to every creature. He that believeth and is baptized shall be saved; but he that believeth*

Muckish, Co. Donegal

Foxglove growing against ancient bee-hive house in Co. Kerry

not shall be condemned. And again: *This Gospel of the kingdom shall be preached in the whole world for a testimony to all nations, and then shall come the end.*

And so too the Lord announces through the prophet, and says: *And it shall come to pass, in the last days, saith the Lord, I will pour out of my Spirit upon all flesh; and your sons and your daughters shall prophesy, and your young men shall see visions, and your old men shall dream dreams. And upon my servants indeed, and upon my handmaids will I pour out in those days of my Spirit, and they shall prophesy.*

And in Hosea He says: *'I will call that which was not my people, my people; ... and her that had not obtained mercy one that hath obtained mercy. And it shall be in the place where it was said: You are not my people. There they shall be called the sons of the living God.'*

Hence, how did it come to pass in Ireland that those who never had a knowledge of God, but until now always worshipped idols and things impure, have now been made a people of the Lord, and are called sons of God, that the sons and daughters of the Kings of the Irish are seen to be monks and virgins of Christ?

Among others, a blessed Irish woman of noble birth, beautiful, full-grown, whom I had baptized, came to us after some days for a particular reason: she told us that she had received a message from a messenger of God, and he admonished her to be a virgin of Christ and draw near to God. Thanks be to God, on the sixth day after this she most laudable and eagerly chose what all virgins of Christ do.

Not that their fathers agree with them; no - they often even suffer persecution and undeserved reproaches from their parents; and yet their number is ever increasing. How many have been reborn there so as to be of our kind, I do not know - not to mention widows and those who practice continence.

But greatest is the suffering of those women who live in slavery. All the time they have to endure terror and threats. But the Lord gave His grace to many of His maidens; for, though they are forbidden to do so, they follow Him bravely.

Wherefore, then, even if I wished to leave them and go to Britain - and how I would have loved to go to my country and my parents, and also to Gaul in order to visit the brethren and to see the face of the saints of my Lord! God knows it that I much desired it; but I am bound by the Spirit, who gives evidence against me if I do this, telling me that I shall be guilty; and I am afraid of losing the labour which I have begun - nay, not I, but Christ the Lord who bade me come here and stay with them for the rest of my life, if the Lord will, and will guard me from every evil way that I may not sin before Him.

This, I presume, I ought to do, but I do not trust myself as long as I am in this body of death, for strong is he who daily strives to turn me away from the faith and the purity of true religion to which I have devoted myself to the end of my life to Christ my Lord. But the hostile flesh is ever dragging us unto death, that is, towards the forbidden satisfaction of one's desires; and I know that in part I did not lead a perfect life as did the other faithful; but I acknowledge it to my Lord, and do not blush before Him, because I lie not: from the time I came to know Him in my youth, the love of God and the fear of Him have grown in me, and up to now, thanks to the grace of God, I have kept the faith.

And let those who will, laugh and scorn - I shall not be silent; nor shall I hide the signs and wonders which the Lord has shown me many years before they came to pass, as He knows everything even before the times of the world.

Hence I ought unceasingly to give thanks to God who often pardoned my folly and my carelessness, and on more than one occasion spared His great wrath on me, who was chosen to be His helper and who was slow to do as was shown me and as the Spirit suggested. And the Lord had mercy on me thousands and thousands of times because He saw that I was ready, but that I did not know what to do in the circumstances. For many tried to prevent this my mission; they would even talk to each other behind my back and say: 'Why does this fellow throw himself into danger among enemies who have no knowledge of God?' It was not malice, but it did not appeal to them because - and to this I own myself - of my rusticity. And I did not realize at once the grace that was then in me; now I understand that I should have done so before.

Now I have given a simple account to my brethren and fellow servants who have believed me because of what I said and still say in order to strengthen and confirm your faith. Would that you, too, would strive for greater things and do better! This will be my glory, for a wise son is the glory of his father.

You know, and so does God, how I have lived among you from my youth in the true faith and in sincerity of heart. Likewise, as regards the heathen among whom I live, I have been faithful to them, and so I shall be. God knows it, I have overreached none of them, nor would I think of doing so, for the sake of God and His Church, for fear of raising persecution against them and all of us, and for fear that through me the name of the Lord be blasphemed; for it is written: *Woe to the man through whom the name of the Lord be blasphemed.*

For although I be rude in all things, nevertheless I have tried somehow to keep myself safe, and that, too, for my Christian brethren, and the virgins of Christ, and the pious women who of their own accord made me gifts and laid on the altar some of their ornaments; and I gave them back to them, and they were offended that I did so. But I did it for the hope of lasting success - in order to preserve myself cautiously in everything so that they might not seize upon me or the ministry of my service, under the pretext of dishonesty, and that I would not even in the smallest matter give the infidels an opportunity to defame or defile.

When I baptized so many thousands of people, did I perhaps expect from any of them as much as half a scruple? Tell me, and I will restore it to you. Or when the Lord ordained clerics everywhere through my unworthy person and I conferred the ministry upon them free, if I asked any of them as much as the price of my shoes, speak against me and I will return it to you.

On the contrary, I spent money for you that they might receive me; and I went to you and everywhere for your sake in many dangers, even to the farthest districts, beyond which there lived nobody and where nobody had ever come to baptize, or to ordain clergy, or to confirm the people. With the grace of the Lord, I did everything lovingly and gladly for your salvation.

All the while I used to give presents to the kings, besides the fees I paid to their sons who travel with me. Even so they laid hands on me and my companions, and on that day they eagerly wished to kill me; but my time had not yet come. And everything they found with us they took away and me they put in irons; and on the fourteenth day the Lord delivered me from their power, and our belongings were returned to us because of God and our dear friends whom we had seen before.

You know how much I paid to those who administered justice in all those districts to which I came frequently. I think I distributed among them not less than the price of fifteen men, so that you might enjoy me, and I might always enjoy you in God. I am not sorry for it - indeed it is not enough for me; I still spend and shall spend more. God has power to grant me afterwards that I myself may be spent for your souls.

Indeed, I call God to witness upon my soul that I lie not; neither, I hope, am I writing to you in order to make this an occasion of flattery or covetousness, nor because I look for honour from any of you. Sufficient is the honour that is not yet seen but is anticipated in the heart. Faithful is He that promised; He never lieth.

But I see myself exalted even in the present world beyond measure by the Lord, and I was not worthy nor such that He should grant me this. I know perfectly well, though not by my own judgment, that poverty and misfortune becomes me better than riches and pleasures. For Christ the Lord, too, was poor for our sakes; and I unhappy wretch that I am, have no wealth even if I wished for it. Daily I expect murder, fraud, or captivity, or whatever it may be; but I fear none of these things because of the promises of heaven. I have cast myself into the hands of God Almighty, who rules everywhere, as the prophet says: *Cast thy thought upon God, and He shall sustain thee.*

So now I commend my soul to my faithful God, for whom I am an ambassador in all my wretchedness; but God accepteth no person, and chose me for this office - to be, although among His least, one of His ministers.

Hence let me render unto Him for all He has done to me. But what can I say or what can I promise to my Lord, as I can do nothing that He has not given me? May He search the hearts and reins; for greatly and exceedingly do I wish, and ready I was, that He should give me His chalice to drink, as He gave it also to the others who loved Him.

Wherefore may God never permit it to happen to me that I should lose His people which He purchased in the utmost parts of the world. I pray to God to give me perseverance and to deign that I be a faithful witness to Him to the end of my life for my God.

And if ever I have done any good for my God whom I love, I beg him to grant me that I may shed my blood with those exiles and captives for His name, even though I should be denied a grave, or my body be woefully torn to pieces limb by limb by hounds or wild beasts, or the fowls of the air devour it. I am firmly convinced that if this should happen to me, I would have gained my soul together with my body, because on that day without doubt we shall rise in the brightness of the sun, that is, in the glory of Christ Jesus our Redeemer, as sons of the living God and joint heirs with Christ, to be made conformable to His image; for of Him, and by Him, and in Him we shall reign.

For this sun which we see rises daily for us because He commands so, but it will never reign, nor will its splendour last; what is more, those wretches who adore it will be miserably punished. Not so we, who believe in, and worship, the true sun - Christ - who will never perish, nor will he who doeth His will; but he will abide for ever as Christ abideth for ever, who reigns with God the Father Almighty and the Holy Spirit before time, and now, and in all eternity. Amen.

Behold again and again would I set forth the words of my confession. I testify in truth and in joy of heart before God and His holy angels that I never had any reason except the Gospel and its promises why I should ever return to the people from whom once before I barely escaped.

I pray those who believe and fear God, whosoever deigns to look at or receive this writing which Patrick, a sinner, unlearned, has composed in Ireland, that no one should ever say that it was my ignorance if I did or showed forth anything however small according to God's good pleasure; but let this be your conclusion and let it so be thought, that - as is the perfect truth - it was the gift of God. This is my confession before I die.

Letter to Coroticus

 Patrick, a sinner, unlearned, resident in Ireland, declare myself to be a bishop. Most assuredly I believe that what I am I have received from God. And so I live among barbarians, a stranger and exile for the love of God. He is witness that this is so. Not that I wished my mouth to utter anything so hard and harsh; but I am forced by the zeal for God; and the truth of Christ has wrung it from me, out of love for my neighbours and sons for whom I gave up my country and parents and my life to the point of death. If I be worthy, I live for my God to teach the heathen, even though some may despise me.

With my own hand I have written and composed these words, to be given, delivered, and sent to the soldiers of Coroticus; I do not say, to my fellow citizens, or to fellow citizens of the holy Romans, but to fellow citizens of the demons, because of their evil works. Like our enemies, they live in death, allies of the Scots and the apostate Picts.

Dripping with blood, they welter in the blood of innocent Christians, whom I have begotten into the number for God and confirmed in Christ!

The day after the newly baptised, anointed with chrism, in white garments (had been slain) - the fragrance was still on their foreheads when they were butchered and slaughtered with the sword by the above-mentioned people - I sent a letter with a holy presbyter whom I had taught from his childhood, clerics accompanying him, asking them to let us have some of the booty, and of the baptised they had made captives. They only jeered at them.

Hence I do not know what to lament more: those who have been slain, or those whom they have taken captive, or those whom the devil has mightily ensnared. Together with him they will be slaves in hell in an eternal punishment; for who committeth sin is a slave and will be called a son of the devil.

Wherefore let every God-fearing man know that they are enemies of me and of Christ my God, for whom I am an ambassador. Parricide! fratricide! ravening wolves that eat the people of the Lord as they eat bread! As is said, the wicked, O Lord, have destroyed Thy law, which but recently He had excellently and kindly planted in Ireland, and which has established itself by the grace of God.

I make no false claim. I share in the work of those whom He called and predestinated to preach the Gospel amidst grave persecutions unto the end of the earth, even if the enemy shows his jealousy through the tyranny of

Coroticus, a man who has no respect for God nor for His priests whom He chose, giving them the highest, divine, and sublime power, that whom they should bind upon earth should be bound also in heaven.

Wherefore, then, I plead with you earnestly, ye holy and humble of heart, it is not permissible to court the favour of such people, nor to take food or drink with them, nor even to accept their alms, until they make reparation to God in hardships, through penance, with shedding of tears, and set free the baptised servants of God and handmaids of Christ, for whom He died and was crucified.

The most High disapproveth the gifts of the wicked … he that offereth sacrifice of the goods of the poor, is as one that sacrificeth the son in the presence of his father. The riches, it is written, which he has gathered unjustly, shall be vomited up from his belly; the angel of death drags him away, by the fury of dragons he shall be tormented, the viper's tongue shall kill him, unquenchable fire devoureth him. And so - woe to those who fill themselves with what is not their own; or, what doth it profit a man that he gain the whole world, and suffer the loss of his own soul?

It would be too tedious to discuss and set forth everything in detail, to gather from the whole Law testimonies against such greed. Avarice is a deadly sin. Thou shalt not covet thy neighbour's goods. Thou shalt not kill. A murderer cannot be with Christ. Whosoever hateth his brother is accounted a murderer. Or, he that loveth not his brother abideth in death. How much more guilty is he that has stained his hands with blood of the sons of God whom He has of late purchased in the utmost part of the earth through the call of our littleness!

Did I come to Ireland without God, or according to the flesh? Who compelled me? I am bound by the Spirit not to see any of my kinsfolk. Is it of my own doing that I have holy mercy on the people who once took me captive and made away with the servants and maids of my father's house? I was freeborn according to the flesh. I am the son of a decurion. But I sold my noble rank - I am neither ashamed nor sorry - for the good of others. Thus I am a servant in Christ to a foreign nation for the unspeakable glory of life everlasting which is in Christ Jesus our Lord.

And if my own people do not know me, a prophet has no honour in his own country. Perhaps we are not of the same fold and have not one and the same God as father, as is written: he that is not with me, is against me, and he that gathereth not with me, scattereth. It is not right that one destroyeth, another buildeth up. I seek not the things that are mine.

It is not my grace, but God who has given this solicitude into my heart, to be one of His hunters or fishers whom God once foretold would come in the last days. I am hated. What shall I do, Lord? I am most despised. Look, Thy sheep around me are torn to pieces and driven away, and that by those robbers, by the orders of the hostile-minded Coroticus. Far from the love of God is a man who hands over Christians to the Picts and Scots. Ravening wolves have devoured the flock of the Lord, which in

Ireland was indeed growing splendidly with the greatest care; and the sons and daughters of kings were monks and virgins of Christ - I cannot count their number. Wherefore, be not pleased with the wrong done to the just; even to hell it shall not please.

Who of the saints would not shudder to be merry with such persons or to enjoy a meal with them? They have filled their houses with the spoils of dead Christians, they live on plunder. They do not know, the wretches, that what they offer their friends and sons as food is deadly poison, just as Eve did not understand that it was death she gave to her husband. So are all that do evil: they work death as their eternal punishment.

This is the custom of the Roman Christians of Gaul: they send holy and able men to the Franks and other heathen with so many thousand solidi to ransom baptised captives. You prefer to kill and sell them to a foreign nation that has no knowledge of God. You betray the members of Christ as it were into a brothel. What hope have you in God, or anyone who thinks as you do, or converses with you in words of flattery? God will judge. For Scripture says: not only they that do evil are worthy to be condemned, but they also that consent to them.

I do not know what I should say or speak further about the departed ones of the sons of God, whom the sword has touched all too harshly. For Scripture says: Weep with them that weep; and again: If one member be grieved, let all members grieve with it. Hence the Church mourns and laments her sons and daughters whom the sword has not yet slain, but who were removed and carried off to faraway lands, where sin abounds openly, grossly, impudently. There people who were freeborn have been sold, Christians made slaves, and that, too, in the service of the abominable, wicked, and apostate Picts!

Therefore I shall raise my voice in sadness and grief: O you fair and beloved brethren and sons whom I have begotten in Christ, countless of number, what can I do you for? I am not worthy to come to the help of God or men. The wickedness of the wicked hath prevailed over us. We have been made, as it were, strangers. Perhaps they do not believe that we have received one and the same baptism, or have one and the same God as father. For them it is a disgrace that we are Irish. Have ye not, as is written, one God? Have ye, every one of you, forsaken his neighbour?

Therefore I grieve for you, I grieve, my dearly beloved. But again, I rejoice within myself. I have not laboured for nothing, and my journeying abroad has not been in vain. And if this horrible, unspeakable crime did happen - thanks be to God, you have left the world and have gone to Paradise as baptised faithful. I see you: you have begun to journey where night shall be no more, nor mourning, nor death; but you shall leap like calves loosened from their bonds, and you shall tread down the wicked, and they shall be ashes under your feet.

You, then, will reign with the apostles, and prophets, and martyrs. You will take possession of eternal kingdoms, as He Himself testifies, saying: They shall come from the east and from the west, and shall sit down with Abraham, and Isaac, and Jacob in the kingdom of heaven. Without are dogs, and sorcerers ... and murderers; and liars and perjurers have their portion in the pool of everlasting fire. Not without reason does the Apostle say: Where the just man shall scarcely be saved, where shall the sinner and ungodly transgressor of the law find himself?

Where, then, will Coroticus with his criminals, rebels against Christ, where will they see themselves, they who distribute baptised women as prizes - for a miserable temporal kingdom, which will pass away in a moment? As a cloud, or smoke that is dispersed by the wind, so shall the deceitful wicked perish at the presence of the Lord; but the just shall feast with great constancy with Christ, they shall judge nations, and rule over wicked kings for ever and ever. Amen.

I testify before God and His angels that it will be so as He indicated to my ignorance. It is not my words that I have set forth in Latin, but those of God and the apostles and prophets, who have never lied. He that believeth shall be saved; but he that believeth not shall be condemned, God hath spoken.

I ask earnestly that whoever is a willing servant of God be a carrier of this letter, so that on no account it be suppressed or hidden by anyone, but rather be read before all the people, and in the presence of Coroticus himself. May God inspire them sometime to recover their senses for God, repenting, however late, their heinous deeds - murderers of the brethren of the Lord! - and to set free the baptised women whom they took captive, in order that they may deserve to live to God, and be made whole, here and in eternity! Be peace to the Father, and to the Son, and to the Holy Spirit. Amen.